Persuasive Speaking and Writing

by Loraine Hoffman

illustrated by Lucas Soeken

cover illustration by John Carrozza

Notice! Copies of student pages may be reproduced by the classroom teacher for classroom use only, not for commercial resale. No part of this publication may be reproduced for storage in a retrieval system, or transmitted in any form or by any means–electronic, mechanical, recording, etc.–without the prior written permission of the publisher. Reproduction of these materials for an entire school or school system is strictly prohibited.

FS-10207 Persuasive Speaking and Writing
All rights reserved–Printed in the U.S.A.
Copyright © 1996 Frank Schaffer Publications, Inc.
23740 Hawthorne Blvd.
Torrance, CA 90505

Introduction

Students employ a wide variety of persuasive techniques all the time. They use these techniques with their friends, siblings, parents, teachers, or other people they interact with.

This resource book offers the teacher a wide range of oral and written language activities that will help students develop persuasive techniques. Additionally, there are activities intended to help students recognize the use of persuasive techniques. This is important since students encounter the use of persuasion in social situations and in advertisements.

Each chapter in this book highlights a specific technique of persuasion. After students have worked through the activities, they will be able to select from many different techniques when they need to speak or write persuasively.

Advertising as a form of persuasion is integrated into the chapters of this book. Students will gain the ability to identify the persuasive techniques used in advertising as they come into contact with them in real-life situations. Examples of persuasion in advertising are used to support the learning process and to reveal to students the relevancy of the material.

The chapters in this text follow a set format. Each chapter begins with an introduction/explanation of a persuasive technique and notes to the teacher regarding each activity in the chapter. The last two activities in each chapter include a critical thinking activity and an integrating activity. The integrating activity is intended to incorporate the newly learned persuasive technique into the genre of persuasion as a whole. The final chapter in this book was created to help students organize their thoughts and ideas for writing a persuasive essay. Tips for persuasive writing are included.

The author wishes to thank Linda Smith for all of her help and Greg Phillips for his encouraging support.

> NOTES TO THE TEACHER

Supporting Evidence

This chapter has been designed to give students a foundation for using all kinds of persuasive techniques when supporting an argument or belief. It is important to help students think about why one viewpoint is favored over another and why some arguments are better than others. Perhaps it is because the speaker or writer uses facts, examples, expert opinions, logic, and emotional appeals. Arguments that we agree with tend to include these five types of evidence. *Facts* are bits of information that can be proven. *Examples* illustrate a case or a point. *Expert opinions* are beliefs by someone who is considered to be experienced in the field. *Logic* is a series of thoughts that lead to a conclusion. *Emotional appeals* build on a person's feelings.

Another technique used in persuasive speaking and writing is refuting. *Refuting* involves looking at opposing viewpoints in an argument and disproving them.

The activities explained below and on page 2 will help students learn to effectively use the types of evidence listed above.

Some of the People Some of the Time (page 3)
Explain to students the five types of evidence mentioned above. Point out that politicians use these techniques all the time in speeches, especially during campaigns. Seek out examples of this in the media. Record a political speech on video. Have students search for evidence and list it on a chart labeled with the five types of evidence. When students have completed this, divide them into groups of four and have them share and compare their findings.

Throw Your Hat in the Ring (page 4)
Invite students to hold a mock election in class. The four offices are president, vice-president, secretary, and treasurer. Brainstorm the important roles of each of the offices. Use this information as part of the evidence students will need in developing their arguments. Divide the class into four groups so that everyone in group one is running for president, everyone in group two is running for vice-president, everyone in group three is running for secretary, and everyone in group four is running for treasurer. Ask each student to write a two-minute campaign speech so that his or her classmates will be convinced to vote for him or her. Regroup students so that each group includes one candidate for each office. Have the students share their speeches in these groups.

Follow-up: Ask students to share their speeches with the entire class. Actually hold mock elections to determine the officers!

Give Me One Good Reason (page 5)
Ask students to think about the conversations they have with their parents when they are trying to persuade them on an issue. Using the five types of evidence discussed, ask students to write scripts for conversations they have to convince their parents to let them go to an amusement park with a school group and to help pay the cost.

Refuting (page 6)

Refuting is the process of disproving an opposing point. In order to refute an argument, it is necessary to be able to see both sides of the issue. That is why it is important to be able to "play the devil's advocate." Discuss the term *devil's advocate* with the students. Have them think of a time when they played this role. Encourage the students to evaluate the pros and cons of issues before judging them.

Critical Thinking and Supporting Evidence—Who Done it? (page 7)

In this scenario, students need to use deductive reasoning skills to identify a thief after looking at the supporting evidence. Evidence is presented for students so that they can determine the significant evidence and then ignore the useless information.

Integrating Supporting Evidence—Dueling Debaters (pages 8 and 9)

Prepare the class for a debate. One suggestion for a topic is the issue of using a rating system for music similar to that used for movies. Of course, other appropriate topics are fine!

If you choose the music rating issue, ask students to get into groups to brainstorm the pros of music rating. Also, tell students to "play the devil's advocate" as well and brainstorm the cons of music rating. Help students think of all the pertinent issues relating to the topic.

Next, divide the class into three groups. One debate group must argue in favor of music rating. The second debate group must argue against music rating. After the formal class debate is held, the third group will decide which group was the most persuasive and identify what that group did that made the arguments so believable. To facilitate this process, group three should use the debate evaluation form (page 9) to record strong evidence presented by the debate teams.

Follow-up: Ask group three to come to a consensus about the winning debate team. Its decision must be supported by solid evidence. A spokesperson from group three must relate and justify the results.

Name _____

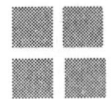

Some of the People Some of the Time

A strong argument has solid supporting evidence. Evidence includes facts, logic, examples, expert opinions, and emotional appeals. It is best when several different types of evidence can be incorporated into an argument.

Politicians are very good at using all kinds of supporting evidence in speeches, particularly during campaigns. Watch a recorded political speech and write down specific examples of the various techniques used by the politician.

EVIDENCE SEARCH

Facts   **Examples**   **Expert Opinions**

_____ _____ _____
_____ _____ _____
_____ _____ _____
_____ _____ _____
_____ _____ _____

Emotional Pleas   **Logic**

_____ _____
_____ _____
_____ _____
_____ _____
_____ _____

Did the speaker rely on one technique more than the others? Which one?
_____
_____

Which argument used the best, most thorough supporting evidence? Why was it the best?
_____
_____

What evidence presented by the politician was the weakest?
_____
_____

Was the speaker successful in using supporting evidence?
_____
_____

Name _____

Throw Your Hat in the Ring

The class is holding elections for president, vice-president, secretary, and treasurer. After selecting the office for which you would like to run, write a two-minute campaign speech to present to your classmates. Be certain to include supporting evidence such as facts, examples, expert opinions, logic, and emotional appeals.

_____
(Office)

_____
_____
_____
_____
_____
_____
_____
_____
_____
_____
_____
_____
_____
_____
_____
_____
_____
_____
_____
_____
_____
_____

Give Me One Good Reason

Pretend that you want to go on a trip to an amusement park with a school group. You must ask your parents for permission and get their help in covering the costs.

Write a script for a conversation you might have with your parents to persuade them to let you go to the amusement park. Be certain to include facts, examples, expert opinions, logic, and emotional appeals in your presentation. Think about how you and your parents would act and react during the conversation.

Refuting

Refuting an argument means bringing up the opposite point of view and then disproving it point by point. In order to refute an argument, you have to know both sides of the issue. That is why it is important to determine the pros and cons of an issue and to learn to "play the devil's advocate."

Think of an issue, such as whether or not communities should set a curfew for their youth. Brainstorm by yourself or in a group all the pros and cons of the issue.

Pros	Cons
_____	_____
_____	_____
_____	_____
_____	_____
_____	_____

Why does it seem that one side of the issue is stronger than the other?
_____
_____
_____
_____

Choose an opposing point of your argument and refute it.
_____
_____
_____
_____
_____

How does refuting that point strengthen your argument?
_____
_____
_____
_____

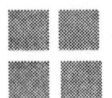

Critical Thinking and Supporting Evidence
—Who Done It?

Sherlock was awakened late Friday night to investigate a baffling robbery scene. It seems a middle school teacher had been burglarized. At the scene of the crime, no fingerprints were found, but the forensic experts located a few possible clues. The forensic experts located some tissue samples where the burglar had bumped into the corner of the desk, leaving some blood. They had also picked up some strands of hair from the crime scene. The last puzzling piece of evidence was a red grade book that was found discarded outside on the lawn. It seems the culprit had been after the teacher's green grade book and had mistakenly grabbed the wrong book.

A week later Sherlock found four likely suspects: Jimmy, Sue, Karen, and Robin. Unfortunately, he did not have enough evidence to hold them. Jimmy's father, a lawyer, had shown up and demanded the release of his son and the other three suspects. Sherlock had stalled as long as he could and was about to order their release when the forensic report came in. As he read the report, his smile grew wider. It seems the assailant had blood type O, was female, and had dark hair. As he pondered, he got out his pencil and scribbled one more clue—red-green colorblindness. Evidently, the culprit could not distinguish between those two colors. Sherlock called up the record division and had them send over the four suspects' files. This is what he found.

> All four had blood type O. Jimmy, Karen, and Robin had brown or dark hair. Using color-blind testing charts, it was determined that Sue and Robin were not colorblind.

With a feeling of satisfaction, Sherlock called the desk sergeant and told him that three of the suspects were innocent, but that the fourth should be charged with the crime.

Who committed the crime?
_____
_____

What is the evidence?
_____
_____

Did Sherlock follow any hunches that proved true? If so, what were they?
_____
_____
_____
_____

© Frank Schaffer Publications, Inc.   7   FS-10207 Persuasive Speaking and Writing

Integrating Supporting Evidence

Dueling Debaters

Your class will have a debate. With your teacher's help, the class should select an appropriate topic to debate. One topic could be whether or not music should have ratings similar to movie ratings. To follow this example, part of the class will argue for ratings, and part of the class will argue against ratings. To prepare for such a debate, brainstorm in groups the pros of the argument. Then, play the devil's advocate and brainstorm as many cons as you can.

Pros	Cons
_____	_____
_____	_____
_____	_____
_____	_____
_____	_____
_____	_____
_____	_____

Refute a point in your "cons" column. Be certain to disprove it.

_____
_____
_____
_____
_____
_____

How does this technique weaken the con argument?

_____
_____
_____
_____
_____
_____

Name _____

Debate Evaluation Form

Evaluate the arguments of the two debate teams. Be certain to look for and record facts, examples, expert opinions, logic, and emotional appeals.

Pro Team Evidence	**Con Team Evidence**
_____	_____
_____	_____
_____	_____
_____	_____
_____	_____
_____	_____
_____	_____
_____	_____
_____	_____
_____	_____
_____	_____
_____	_____

Which team's evidence was more convincing? Why?
_____
_____
_____
_____

Who won the debate? _____

Explain the reasons for your decision.
_____
_____
_____
_____

NOTES TO THE TEACHER
The Bandwagon Technique

When the bandwagon technique is used, people are persuaded to do something, think something, or buy something just because other people are doing, thinking, or buying it. "Everybody else wears designer jeans" is an example of the bandwagon technique. People are persuaded to "jump on the bandwagon" and buy a pair of designer jeans. Another example of jumping on the bandwagon would be if many students have a particular brand of backpack, and someone wants one just because the others have it.

Advertisers use the bandwagon approach often because they hope that an item's popularity will help sell it. Indeed, the idea works! Look at how the popularity of small plastic building blocks, pagers, and cellular phones has grown, largely because many people have them.

It is important to remember that the truth of an idea is not necessarily related to its popularity. Just because many people share a certain belief does not mean that the belief is correct and accurate. The same goes with purchases. People may buy something not because they need it, but because they liked what someone else had.

The most common and effective uses of the bandwagon technique are in commercials and advertising. Saying that "four out of five dentists surveyed recommend" a certain toothpaste is an example of the bandwagon technique. A person may be persuaded to buy that particular brand of toothpaste because so many dentists think it is the best. Actually, the consumer does not know how many dentists were surveyed, how they were surveyed, or who selected the dentists who were surveyed. The company selling the toothpaste is simply using the bandwagon technique to make people believe that most dentists would recommend its brand of toothpaste.

After the students are familiar with the bandwagon technique, let them try the activities described below.

Air Wave Ads (page 13)
A restaurant chain has counted how many customers have been served. If a sign says, "14 billion served," then that restaurant must cook great hamburgers! The restaurant wants others to jump on the bandwagon and buy some of their hamburgers, too.

Perhaps a restaurant advertises its popularity by suggesting that "everyone" goes there! Customers patronize the restaurant because they want to be a part of a group and see "everyone." Ask students to imagine that they are in charge of advertising for Pete's Pizza Parlor. Tell them they are going to create a 45-second radio advertisement to persuade people to eat at Pete's Pizza Parlor. Each student should create his or her own ad.

After students have written their radio spots for Pete's Pizza Parlor, have them work in groups of four to practice them. Encourage group members to help one another with content, tone, and style. For added fun, tape-record the radio commercials and play them back.

Snap, Crackle, Purchase! (pages 14 and 15)

Breakfast cereal is a big business! One commercial advertises, "Unless they're weird, your kids will like it!" This example of the bandwagon technique is easy to remember and convinces consumers that the cereal tastes good!

To check for understanding, ask students in large or small groups to brainstorm examples of commercials that employ the bandwagon technique of persuasion. Students must be able to explain how the commercial encourages everyone to "jump on the bandwagon."

Ask students to make up a new cereal, name it, and designate target consumers. Tell students that they will write a 60-second script for a television commercial.

Enrich the 60-second television cereal commercial script by designing a graphic that can be used on a billboard or in a magazine advertisement.

The Latest Fad! (page 16)

Ask students to make a list of four current fads. Discuss with students how fads begin, as well as why they come about. Why do people love fads so much? How and why do certain fads become so popular?

Have students explain in detail why certain fads are popular today. Use students' explanations to create a lively classroom discussion about fads.

The Bandwagon and You! (page 17)

Ask students to think about times when they used the bandwagon technique to convince their parents to buy something. Invite students to share their examples with the class. Then take a class vote to see if several students in the class convinced their parents to purchase some of the same items for the same reasons.

The Bandwagon and Critical Thinking (page 18)

Remind students that what is popular and what they truly think, believe, or need are not always the same thing. Buying something just because someone else has it is not always the best thing! Students should remember that they have minds of their *own,* and jumping on the bandwagon every time it comes by is not always the smartest idea. Ask students to write about a time when jumping on the bandwagon was not a good idea.

Integrating the Bandwagon Technique (pages 19 and 20)

Use cooperative groups of four to integrate the bandwagon technique. Each group is to create a television commercial for a product that the group designs. The group should complete the following:

1. the product (made to actual size)
2. the marketing background (answers to questions 1-7 below)
3. the script for the commercial
4. the graphic (magazine or billboard advertisement)

Prepare students for writing television commercials by letting them watch several that you have taped. Select commercials that incorporate the bandwagon technique. Students need to look for product ideas and techniques of persuasion, particularly the bandwagon technique. Students should write down their ideas and observations on the *Television Commercial Observation Form* (page 19).

In their cooperative groups, students should answer the following questions and complete the "Marketing Background" activity sheet (page 20). The answers will help students write their television commercials.

1. Name your product. Explain why is it used.
2. What are three reasons to buy this product?
3. How much does the product cost?
4. Where will the product be sold?
5. Who are your target consumers?
6. Think of a strategy for your commercial to get and maintain our attention.
7. Make up a little song, jingle, or rap that will help sell your product.

After answering the questions, each group should design its product at actual size, write a script for the commercial which will include the jingle or rap, and design a graphic for use in magazine and billboard advertising.

Follow-Up: Have the groups act out their commercials for the class. Videotape them for fun! If video equipment is not available, perhaps you could take a snapshot of each group with its product and advertisement.

Lights, Action, Enrichment (page 21)

As the groups are watching one another's commercials (either live or on videotape), ask students to write down the types of evidence used by each group. Also, ask them to identify and write down examples of the bandwagon approach to persuasion that are used.

Air Wave Ads

Some restaurants advertise the number of people they have served. They want you to think that if that many people have eaten at the restaurant, then the food must be really good! They hope that you will "jump on the bandwagon" and eat at the restaurant too! A restaurant may advertise, "Eat at Chet's Chicken Shack, the cool after-school snack shop!" The advertisers hope you will eat there after school because "everyone" will be there. These are examples of using the bandwagon technique to persuade people to eat at particular restaurants. Imagine that you are in charge of advertising for Pete's Pizza Parlor. You decide to put a radio advertisement on the most popular radio station to boost business. Use what you know about the bandwagon technique of persuasion to write a 45-second radio spot that will convince people to eat pizza at Pete's Pizza Parlor.

_____
_____
_____
_____
_____
_____
_____
_____
_____
_____
_____
_____
_____
_____
_____
_____
_____
_____
_____
_____
_____

Name _____

◫ *Snap, Crackle, Purchase!*

Selling cereal is big business! One commercial sells a cereal by saying, "Unless they're weird, your kids will like it!" This example of the bandwagon technique is easy to remember and convinces consumers that the cereal tastes good.

Create an idea for a new cereal that you think will sell. Give it a name and list its basic ingredients. Think about your target consumers. Is your cereal going to be for kids, athletes, older people, or health-conscious people?

Breakfast cereal name:
_____

For (target consumers):
_____

In the space below, design an advertising graphic that could be used to advertise your new cereal in a magazine advertisement or on a billboard.

Advertising Graphic

Write a 60-second script for a commercial to be aired on television. Be certain to make the cereal sound appealing by using words that show why the consumer should buy the cereal. For example: high fiber, natural, daily allowance of vitamins, low fat, crunchy, great taste, fun, toys inside the box, etc.

The Latest Fad!

As the latest fad gains popularity, everyone jumps on the bandwagon! In the sixties, everybody loved Hula-Hoops. In the eighties, Teenage Mutant Ninja Turtles and Cabbage Patch Kids were the rage. In the early nineties, Power Rangers and the Lion King were popular. Everything from toothbrushes and party supplies to coloring books and cups featured these great fads!

List four current fads.

_____
_____
_____
_____

Explain why these fads are so popular today.

_____
_____
_____
_____

Think about what brings fads into such popularity. Then pretend that the president of a large company wants to meet with you because you have created a product that could become the latest fad. You will need to tell why your fad will help sell the company's product lines. As usual, the executive is very busy and does not have much time. You have 20 seconds to get the president's attention and give an exciting and energized explanation of why your fad is a "fad-tabulous" idea that will sell the company's products!

Why will your fad sell the company's products?

_____
_____
_____
_____
_____
_____
_____
_____

Name _____

The Bandwagon and You!

Have you ever convinced your parents to buy something because it is a popular item to have? Have you ever bought something because an item was popular and you knew several other people who had it?

Think about a time that you convinced your parents to buy something. What was the item? How did you use the bandwagon technique? Maybe you convinced them because a lot of kids in the neighborhood had something and you wanted it too. Maybe the other people who already owned it said it was useful or nice.

Describe in detail an example of when you convinced your parents to buy something because it seemed like a good idea and a lot of other people had it.

_____
_____
_____
_____
_____
_____
_____
_____
_____
_____
_____
_____
_____
_____
_____
_____
_____
_____
_____
_____
_____
_____
_____
_____

The Bandwagon and Critical Thinking

Sometimes the best thing is to NOT jump on the bandwagon. Remember, you have a mind of your own, and even though an idea or an item is popular, that does not guarantee that it is the best idea or item for you! Parents have often been known to ask their kids, "Well if Johnny jumped off a cliff, would you do it too?" But what they really want to know is whether you are thinking for yourself or letting others think for you.

Write a scenario about an individual who should NOT jump on the bandwagon. Explain why the decision is a hard one to make for that individual, and give clear reasons for his or her decision. Make your story shows how important it is for people to think for themselves.

Name _____

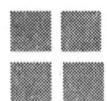

Television Commercial Observation Form

Watch several commercials on television before you write one of your own. What products are being advertised? What techniques are being used to sell the products? Write your observations and comments in the spaces provided.

1. Product _____

Persuasive Techniques Used _____
_____

Comment _____
_____

2. Product _____

Persuasive Techniques Used _____
_____

Comment _____
_____

3. Product _____

Persuasive Techniques Used _____
_____

Comment _____

4. Product _____

Persuasive Techniques Used _____
_____

Comment _____

© Frank Schaffer Publications, Inc.   FS-10207 Persuasive Speaking and Writing

Names _____

Marketing Background

Complete the following marketing questions with your group. Use these ideas for the commercial you are writing with your cooperative group.

1. Name your product. Explain why it is used.
_____
_____

2. What are three reasons to buy your product?
_____
_____
_____
_____

3. How much does the product cost? _____

4. Where will the product be sold?
_____

5. Who are your target consumers?
_____
_____

6. Think of a strategy for your commercial to get and maintain our attention.
_____
_____
_____

7. Make up a little song, jingle, or rap that will help sell your product.
_____
_____

© Frank Schaffer Publications, Inc. FS-10207 Persuasive Speaking and Writing

Name _____

Lights, Action, Enrichment

While you are watching the commercials created by the other groups, look for the types of persuasive evidence that the group members employ to sell their products. Also, identify and write down the bandwagon approach to persuasion whenever you notice it being used. Be certain to list at least one thing that you really liked about each commercial.

Group 1

Bandwagon Technique Used _____

_____

Other Persuasive Techniques Used _____

_____

One thing I liked was _____

_____

Group 2

Bandwagon Technique Used _____

_____

Other Persuasive Techniques Used _____

_____

One thing I liked was _____

_____

Group 3

Bandwagon Technique Used _____

_____

Other Persuasive Techniques Used _____

_____

One thing I liked was _____

_____

Group 4

Bandwagon Technique Used _____

_____

Other Persuasive Techniques Used _____

_____

One thing I liked was _____

_____

© Frank Schaffer Publications, Inc.	FS-10207 Persuasive Speaking and Writing

NOTES TO THE TEACHER
Glittering Generalities

Another way of persuading people to do or believe something is by using *glittering generalities*. A glittering generality is a technique that uses terms or phrases that are vague and general. The terms are so general that they cannot be proven or disproven. Glittering generalities are meant to evoke positive feelings in people. Advertisers try to establish a connection between their products and the positive feelings brought about by certain terms. For instance, "Coke™ is the real thing" is an example of a glittering generality because it makes the consumer feel that the product is the best and the original, which infers that everything else is a substitute. "The real thing" may mean different things to different people.

Another example of a glittering generality is Loving Care Hair Coloring. The glittering generality is in the product name. Consumers feel that their hair will be cared for lovingly if they use that hair color. The name infers that the product will be gentle and will not damage hair.

Politicians running for political offices use many glittering generalities. They may say, "Vote for the future, vote for me!" Voters want a better future, so they may very well give that candidate their votes. It is important to remember, however, that voters are responsible for asking about whose future the candidate will truly endorse.

The activities described below and on pages 23 and 24 will help students recognize glittering generalities and understand how they are used.

Foot Peddlers (page 25)
Encourage students to imagine that they are in charge of sales for a major shoe company that manufactures four types of shoes: ladies' dress shoes, toddlers' shoes, athletic shoes, and boots. Ask students to think of glittering generalities to use for the brand name of each type of shoe. Tell them that they want consumers to feel good about their shoes partly because of the glittering names. Ask students to think of all the qualities they look for in shoes and to use those words in the brand names.

Sparkling Slogans (page 26 and 27)
There are a lot of popular glittering generality phrases. In this activity, students are encouraged to realize that a good glittering generality is so vague and general that it can really be used to describe more than one product. For example, "It just tastes red" could be used for red soda, red candy, red gelatin, or red gum. The explanation would be that people who like red tend to like cherry, strawberry, or cinnamon flavors. Red does not specify any one of these flavors exactly; therefore, it will most likely appeal to all the people who like any one of these flavors. Encourage students to go through this thought process for each glittering generality listed, concentrating on products (either real or invented) that could be sold using these glittering generalities. It may help students to review the example provided on the activity sheet.

Super Shopper (page 28)

Grocery stores frequently market products that use glittering generalities to sell the items. "Fresh" or "fresh squeezed" is an example, since it appeals to our desire for fresh food. After all, it sounds delicious, but one must question how fresh something really is. "Fresh" implies that the item was made a very short time ago, yet we know that the standards of "fresh" vary greatly. "Organic" is another term that is vague, since standards of organic foods vary greatly. Dieters may purchase an item that is "low cal," yet when one reads the label, there are still many calories in the food item. The same phenomenon occurs with the terms "low fat" and "low sodium." "Low Fat" does not tell anything about how many fat grams are actually in the product. These glittering generalities evoke in consumers the feeling that they are selecting food that is appropriate for their diets, when in fact, reading the food labels is the only way to truly know.

Ask students to think of glittering generalities that they might see in a grocery store for the items listed in this activity.

Breakfast Blitz (page 29)

There are many cereals that are named by glittering generalities. Great Grains and Magic Stars are examples that stir positive feelings by the words *great* and *magic*. The answer key for this activity is printed below.

Kids' Cereals		Adults' Cereals	
Yes	Lucky Charms	Yes	Special K
No	Frosted Flakes	No	Corn Flakes
Yes	Life	Yes	Healthy Choice
No	Fruity Pebbles	No	Mini-Wheats
Yes	King Vitamin	No	Raisin Bran
Yes	Golden Grahams	Yes	Basic 4
No	Cocoa Puffs	No	Bran Flakes
No	Count Chocula	Yes	Total

The Bigger the Better (page 30)

Glittering generalities often are used to denote something big. Consumers are persuaded to buy the largest size of various products. But why is it that people feel the need to buy the biggest? Encourage students to explore this question through interviewing others and writing a concise paragraph. It may be that people want more for their money and that they feel they get breaks when they buy the largest. Advertisers zero in on this phenomenon.

Glittering Generalities and Critical Thinking (page 31)
Politicians use glittering generalities as a powerful campaigning tool during reelection periods. "Vote for the future," "Vote for change," "Vote for peace," and "He (or she) will make this country great again!" are all examples of glittering generalities in politics. No one can prove or disprove these statements because they are too vague and general. For this reason, voters must take the responsibility of educating themselves about the candidates. This is an important concept for students to understand.

Have each student pretend that he or she is the campaign manager for someone who is running for president. Ask each student to to write a campaign speech for the presidential candidate, including the basic platform, educational issues, the economy, the budget, and other pertinent issues and current events. In addition, encourage students to select realistic slogans as well as glittering generalities that their candidates might use to promote themselves.

Caped Crusaders (page 32)
The names of superheroes are also glittering generalities which evoke positive feelings from people about the characters. Ask students to select two superheroes from the list provided in this activity, or to think of two of their own, and write a brief description about what makes their superheroes so super.

Integrating Glittering Generalities (page 33)
Ask students to think of their very favorite superheroes, and then pretend that they get to interview them. What questions will the students ask? Encourage students to plan questions about the superhero's childhood, parents, schooling, siblings, etc. Ask students to write this imaginary interview on the activity sheet.

Prepare for a VOTE! (page 34)
As a final activity, ask students to look back at their descriptive essays (page 32) and their mock interviews (page 33). Tell them to pick their very favorite superhero and be prepared to defend him or her. Next, tell students to write a five-sentence paragraph that explains concisely and clearly why their superhero should be voted the best. After each individual has written a paragraph, divide students into groups and allow them to read their paragraphs aloud. The students must be as convincing as possible!

Following a small-group discussion about the most outstanding superhero, the group must vote on the best one. Encourage students to base their votes on the student who was most persuasive, using supporting persuasive evidence and elaborating on other persuasive techniques. Allow each group to share its results with the class by reading the winning paragraph. It may be fun to award small prizes to the winning student from each group!

Name _____

Foot Peddlers

There is a new type of shoe company that is manufacturing four types of shoes. Assume that you have been hired to produce a sales pitch for these shoes. Think about names, words, and phrases that would use glittering generalities to promote the shoe sales. Consider words like *fast*, *comfort*, *jumping*, and *kicking*. For example, some shoe manufacturers use *Easy* in the brand name in an effort to make the shoes sound comfortable. These words make consumers feel good about their shoes. Create a glittering generality brand name for each type of shoe, and write several glittering generality words or phrases that could be used to sell the shoes.

Ladies' Dress Shoes

Brand Name:_____

Descriptive words and phrases:

1. _____
2. _____
3. _____

Toddlers' Shoes

Brand Name:_____

Descriptive words and phrases:

1. _____
2. _____
3. _____

Athletic Shoes

Title: _____

Descriptive words and phrases:

1. _____
2. _____
3. _____

Boots

Title: _____

Descriptive words and phrases:

1. _____
2. _____
3. _____

Name _____

Sparkling Slogans

Many glittering generality phrases could be used for more than one product. Listed below are some glittering generality phrases that have really been used. Recall or invent at least three different products that could be sold using these glittering generalities, and write them in the blanks. Next, write an explanation of how the glittering generality links positive feelings to the product. As an example, the first one has been done for you.

1. "It just tastes red." (Big Red Soda)

| Big Red Soda | Tasty Red Gum | Steamy Red Candy |

Explanations:

People who like strawberry and cherry flavor will like this cream soda.

The big cinnamon flavor of this chewing gum will make your breath fresh.

The red hot flavor of this candy brings your mouth to life.

2. "It does a body good." (milk)

A. _____ B. _____ C. _____

Explanations:

_____ _____ _____
_____ _____ _____
_____ _____ _____

3. "They're Gr-r-r-reat!" (Kellogg's Frosted Flakes)

A. _____ B. _____ C. _____

Explanations:

_____ _____ _____
_____ _____ _____
_____ _____ _____

© Frank Schaffer Publications, Inc.   26   FS-10207 PERSUASIVE Speaking and Writing

4. "It's the real thing." (Coca-Cola)

A. _____ B. _____ C. _____

Explanations:

_____ _____ _____
_____ _____ _____
_____ _____ _____

5. "Don't leave home without it." (American Express)

A. _____ B. _____ C. _____

Explanations:

_____ _____ _____
_____ _____ _____
_____ _____ _____

6. "Leave the driving to us." (Greyhound Bus Lines)

A. _____ B. _____ C. _____

Explanations:

_____ _____ _____
_____ _____ _____
_____ _____ _____

Name _____

Super Shopper

Pretend that your parents sent you to the grocery store to buy some food for the family. Since they recently started diets, they asked you to buy foods that will help to keep them slim and trim. What glittering generalities might you see on the food products you need to buy at the grocery store? Try to recall labels and brands that you have seen for the following items.

Butter or Margarine

1. _____
2. _____
3. _____

Frozen Foods

1. _____
2. _____
3. _____

Cheese

1. _____
2. _____
3. _____

Desserts

1. _____
2. _____
3. _____

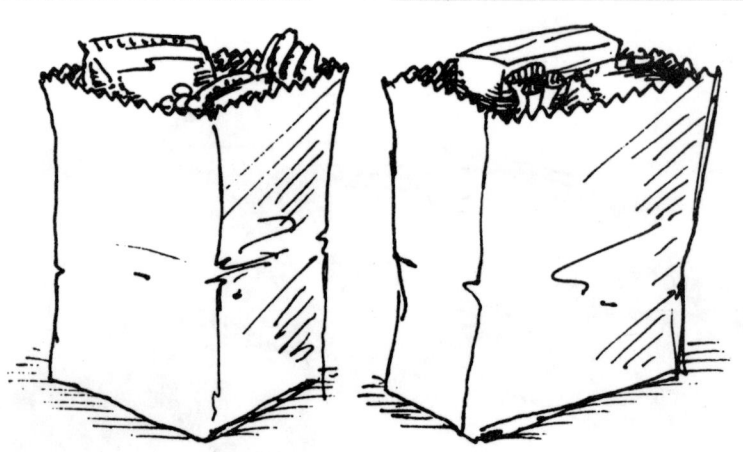

© Frank Schaffer Publications, Inc. FS-10207 Persuasive Speaking and Writing

Name _____

Breakfast Blitz

Different cereals have different target consumers. Some cereals appeal to kids, and their advertisements sometimes offer prizes that are free with a purchase. Some cereals appeal to those who want fiber in their diet, like All-Bran and Fibre One. One cereal advertises that it is the breakfast of champions. Remember that even product names can be glittering generalities if they evoke positive feelings in the consumer. Look at the cereals listed below. Write *YES* beside the cereal name if it is a glittering generality. Write *NO* if it is not a glittering generality. Then add two more glittering generality cereal names to each column. You may make them up or use product names that you have seen in the store.

Kids' Cereals	Adults' Cereals
____ Lucky Charms	____ Special K
____ Frosted Flakes	____ Corn Flakes
____ Life	____ Healthy Choice
____ Fruity Pebbles	____ Mini-Wheats
____ King Vitamin	____ Raisin Bran
____ Golden Grahams	____ Basic 4
____ Cocoa Puffs	____ Bran Flakes
____ Count Chocula	____ Total

1. _____   1. _____
2. _____   2. _____

Challenge
Choose one of the cereals that does not have a glittering generality in its name. Add a word or phrase that will make it appeal to people's positive feelings.

_____
_____
_____
_____

Name _____

The Bigger the Better

There are a lot of ways to say "BIG." Sometimes sellers want their product consumers to think BIG! Consumers are persuasively encouraged to buy the biggest size, and they keep going for the largest item over and over. These BIG items range broadly, and they come in wide varieties. There are examples in the following list:

    BIGGIE FRIES
    BIG FOOT PIZZA
    BIG GULP (drink)
    MAXIMA (car)
    SUPER TANK (drink)
    DEEP DISH PIZZA
    TACO GRANDE

In this list alone, there are many ways to say "BIG!" Think of some examples that you have seen recently that are examples of glittering generalities that mean big.

1. _____
2. _____
3. _____

Interview a teacher, parent, or friend and ask why he or she thinks people feel it is important to buy big. There must be a market for big items if there are so many glittering generalities that mean big. On the lines below, write several reasons and ideas that were expressed to you during your interview in the space provided.

_____
_____
_____
_____
_____
_____
_____
_____
_____
_____
_____
_____
_____

© Frank Schaffer Publications, Inc.   FS-10207 Persuasive Speaking and Writing

Name _____

Glittering Generalities and Critical Thinking

Politicians running for political office use many glittering generalities during their campaigns. Campaigns are built on phrases such as, "Vote for Change," "Peace," "Vote for the future," and "He (or she) will make this country great again!" But what these glittering generality phrases really mean for voters is oftentimes not known. In other words, the slogan may not make it clear what kind of "change" the voter would be voting for. This is why it is the responsibility of the voters to educate themselves about the candidates.

Pretend that you are the campaign manager for a presidential candidate. Write a brief campaign speech explaining the basic platform of your candidate. What will this candidate represent? Remember to consider education issues, the economy, and the budget. Be certain to include any other pertinent issues or current events of which you are aware. Include a slogan and other glittering generalities to promote your candidate.

_____
_____
_____
_____
_____
_____
_____
_____
_____
_____
_____
_____
_____
_____
_____
_____
_____
_____

Caped Crusaders

Many superheroes have glittering generalities in their names. Listed below are several examples of superheroes whose names include glittering generalities. Select two super heroes from the list, or think of two on your own, and describe in brief essays what makes them superheroes.

Captain America   Greatest American Hero
Fantastic Four   Shazam
Wonder Woman   The Wonder Twins
The Flash   Superman

1. _____

2. _____

Name _____

Integrating Glittering Generalities

Think of your favorite superhero. Pretend that you get to interview him or her. Ask the superhero about life experiences that led him or her to become a superhero. Ask questions about the superhero's childhood, parents, siblings, school, etc. Write your interview questions and the superhero's answers below.

Q: _____

A: _____
_____
_____

Q: _____

A: _____
_____
_____

Q: _____

A: _____
_____
_____

Q: _____

A: _____
_____
_____

Q: _____

A: _____
_____
_____

Name _____

Prepare for a Vote!

Think of your favorite superhero. Look back at the descriptive essays and the interview that you wrote. Write a concise, five-sentence paragraph to persuade your group that your superhero should be voted the best!

_____
_____
_____
_____
_____
_____
_____
_____
_____
_____

After you write your paragraph, meet with your group. Have each group member read his or her concise paragraph, trying to persuade the others in the group to vote for his or her superhero. Following a discussion, your group must vote for the best superhero based on the persuasive paragraphs.

© Frank Schaffer Publications, Inc. FS-10207 Persuasive Speaking and Writing

> **NOTES TO THE TEACHER**

Name-Calling

Name-calling is nearly the opposite of a glittering generality. While glittering generalities evoke positive feelings, name-calling brings out negative images and feelings that people associate with an item, product, or person. Name-calling can be used as a negative form of persuasion. For instance, in a recent American car manufacturer commercial, an American vehicle was compared to its foreign competitor. Since some Americans feel that the foreign car industry may be stealing American jobs and business, the term *foreign* might evoke negative feelings in them, possibly persuading them to buy automobiles made in the USA.

Another example can be seen in fast-food companies and their sales of French fries. Some major hamburger chains sell French fries in various sizes. They have moved away from selling small, medium, and large sizes to selling child-size, small, and regular. It's important to note that the child-size is comparable to the what used to be small, just as the new small equals the old medium. The name-calling is found in the term *child*. Most teenagers and adults would not purchase a child-size, even though the portion has not changed from the old small. The technique is being used to persuade people to buy the next larger size, at a higher cost, because the teenage or adult customer does not want to appear to be childlike.

Political campaign years bring out name-calling among candidates. Such name-calling is often called mudslinging. One candidate may say that the other is "soft" on an issue, implying that the candidate has a weak backbone or cannot make a competent decision on that issue.

Know Your Audience (page 38)
Knowing your audience is critical when using the persuasive technique of name-calling. Two scenarios are listed in this activity to help students begin to see differences in perceptions of common terms. Perspectives change depending on the audience.

It's All in the Way You Look at It (page 39)
This activity asks students to identify various audiences and their perceptions. For example, regarding the word *clown*, a clown in a circus may evoke positive feelings, while a teacher may perceive a class clown with negative feelings. Likewise, a ticket to a concert may be positive, while a ticket for speeding is negative. Students must be able to justify the answers they offer on this activity.

In the Challenge, a typical term that has become popularized among students probably is perceived differently among different people. For example, the term *bad* is sometimes used to describe something that is really neat. Other people perceive the term to mean just that, bad.

Mudslinging (page 40)
Studying an election to understand the name-calling technique provides a wonderful opportunity to get students involved in a current election, or to employ students' research skills by having them go to the library to research newspaper and magazine clippings from a previous election. Ask each student to select an election (past or present), and ask him or her to find at least five examples of name-calling between two candidates running for the same office.

Undermining Advertising (page 41)
Ask students to select an item that is produced by companies that are in competition with one another. Donuts, mouthwash, cheese, and soda are all examples. Students should create advertisements for their items that employ the name-calling technique. They want consumers to choose to buy their product whenever they have to pick up that item at the store. Each advertisement should have a slogan and a logo. The catchy slogan should use name-calling.

Labeling Lowlifes (page 42)
The name-calling persuasive technique can be seen in the names given to the villains that confront superheros. Students will select their favorite superheros, and then invent three different villains that might confront the superheros. The names of the villains should be examples of the name-calling technique.

Roundup Review (page 43)
Glittering generalities and name-calling are nearly opposites. This activity allows students to review the two persuasive techniques. Several terms are listed, and students mark a G if the term is a glittering generality and N if the term is name-calling. The answer key for the activity is shown below.

N	Fence-sitter	N	Litterbug
G	Sparkling Water	G	Computer Wiz
N	Dragon Breath	G	Great Grains Cereal
G	Busy Bee	G	Meaty Bites Dog Food
N	Rug Rat	G	Sweet Corn
G	Baby Soft	N	Cry Baby
N	Grub Worm	N	Pizza Face
N	Fire Ant	G	Mighty Dog

Name-Calling and Critical Thinking: Tabloid Journalism (page 44)
While tabloid newspapers are not necessarily factual, there is still a huge market for them. Discuss with students possible reasons for this. Tabloid journalism often evokes negative feelings and images about people, especially celebrities. Some articles are intended to persuade the reader to distrust or dislike someone or something.

Divide the class into groups of four. Find excerpts from tabloid newspapers that are appropriate for students. Since tabloid journalism does include some material that is inappropriate for children, be sure to carefully screen the articles that you select for use. Perhaps you can select a different article for each group. Have the group members read the group's article together and highlight words or phrases that employ the name-calling technique. The groups will write the words and phrases that are examples of the name-calling technique on the activity sheet.

Integrating Name-Calling: Wanted! **(page 45)**

Tell the students that they will be designing "Wanted" posters. Examples of actual "Wanted" posters are often displayed in U.S. Post Offices. Brainstorm with students about places where they might see posters like these, and discuss important facts that might be included on one. Invite each student to design one of his or her own, including name or aliases, specific description, and the amount of the reward.

Know Your Audience

Name-calling does not always evoke negative images and feelings. Many of the images evoked depend upon the audience. While most glittering generalities typically evoke positive feelings, it is not necessarily true that all name-calling evokes negative feelings. Therefore, it becomes imperative to know your audience when using this persuasive technique.

For example, at a Republican convention, if a speaker is referred to as a "liberal," it might evoke negative feelings in the crowd because the listeners might be conservatives and think that a liberal would want to raise taxes or spend more money. This would be considered name-calling. However, at a Democratic convention, the use of the word *liberal* may not evoke negative feelings or images because the listeners might consider themselves to be liberals.

Below are three scenarios that could involve name-calling. Above each scenario are two words. One of the words is name-calling because it evokes a negative image for certain audiences.

1. Old/Antique
Suzie went home with her friend Mary after school. They decided to sit on the couch to do their homework. Suzie noticed a tear in the fabric of the couch. Mary explained that it was an _____ couch.

2. Northerners/Yankees
A group of students were touring Atlanta, Georgia. During the tour, they were shown many restored buildings from the fires that swept through Atlanta during the Civil War. The tour guide, a native southerner, explained that the city was burned by _____.

3. Peculiar/Weird
Joe's Aunt Sara has a snake collection. More than 30 snakes slither freely around her house. Joe likes the snakes, but he thinks his aunt is _____.

Name _____

It's All in the Way You Look at It

Part of the power of persuasion is strengthened by knowing your audience. Different groups of people perceive different terms in different ways. Name a group or audience that would view each listed word or term as name-calling (negative), and a group that would not.

1. Conservative

Group that would view conservative as negative: _____

Group that would NOT: _____

2. Calories

Group that would view calories as negative: _____

Group that would NOT: _____

3. Drugs

Group that would view drugs as negative: _____

Group that would NOT: _____

4. Ticket

Group that would view ticket as negative: _____

Group that would NOT: _____

5. Clown

Group that would view clown as negative: _____

Group that would NOT: _____

Challenge: Think of an example in your everyday life where a term you use may be viewed negatively by some people, but not by others. Explain the example in the space below.

_____
_____
_____
_____
_____

Name _____

Mudslinging

Mudslinging is a form of name-calling in which politicians make derogatory statements about the opposing candidates or attack the views of their opponents.

For example, one candidate may describe the other as a friend of "big business." This implies that the politician is out of touch with the common people, and that under his/her leadership, the rich people will continue to get richer.

Find local, state, or national election advertisements or information in television commercials or the newspapers. If it is not an election year, go to the library and look up old newspaper articles from a past election.

Select two opposing candidates. On the lines below, list five examples of mudslinging (name-calling) that were said by one candidate about the other. Remember: You are looking for words that evoke negative images or feelings about the opponent.

Election (political race and year): _____

Candidate #1
Name: _____
1. _____
2. _____
3. _____
4. _____
5. _____

Candidate #2
Name: _____
1. _____
2. _____
3. _____
4. _____
5. _____

Which candidate used stronger name-calling language? _____
Which candidate won the election? _____
Why do you think that he or she won? _____
_____
_____

© Frank Schaffer Publications, Inc. FS-10207 Persuasive Speaking and Writing

Name _____

Undermining Advertising

Name-calling is used to downgrade a competitor's product. For instance, a pizza chain tells customers to "Avoid the Noid," implying that the chain delivers hot, appetizing pizza quickly and that other pizza vendors do not. In fact, the worst case scenario may be that the competitors' pizzas may be cold when they arrive.

Another example can be seen in a soft drink manufacturer that calls its product "the uncola." The company claims that its product is caffeine free, has never had caffeine, and never will have caffeine. This implies that other soft drinks have caffeine and must therefore be less desirable.

Select an item, such as bread or toothpaste, that is made by more than one company. In the box below, create an advertisement to persuade consumers not to choose the competitor's product. Instead, convince consumers to purchase your product. Be certain to include a logo and a slogan that employ the name-calling technique in your advertisement.

Name _____

⊞ Labeling Lowlifes

Villains are often given names that evoke negative feelings or images in the audience. This form of name-calling makes the hero look better than the villain. Some famous villains with names that use this form of name-calling are Wolf Man, The Joker, Mr. Freeze, Dr. Doom, Green Goblin, and Scar.

Pretend that your favorite superhero is beset by several new evil villains. Invent names for three new villains who will confront your superhero. Then describe them and explain why each will be an interesting opponent for the superhero.

_____
Favorite Superhero

Villain #1 Name: _____
Physical Description: _____
Why the villain will be a good opponent: _____
_____
_____

Villain #2 Name: _____
Physical Description: _____
Why the villain will be a good opponent: _____
_____
_____

Villain #3 Name: _____
Physical Description: _____
Why the villain will be a good opponent: _____
_____
_____

© Frank Schaffer Publications, Inc.   FS-10207 Persuasive Speaking and Writing

Roundup Review

Name-calling and glittering generalities are nearly opposite persuasive techniques. Listed below are various terms. Some are glittering generalities and some are name-calling. Read each term and write **G** if the term is a glittering generality and **N** if the term is name-calling.

____ Fence-sitter
____ Sparkling Water
____ Dragon Breath
____ Busy Bee
____ Rug Rat
____ Baby Soft
____ Grub Worm
____ Fire Ant

____ Litterbug
____ Computer Wiz
____ Great Grains Cereal
____ Meaty Bites Dog Food
____ Sweet Corn
____ Cry Baby
____ Pizza Face
____ Mighty Dog

What are the most important differences between glittering generalities and name-calling?
_____
_____
_____
_____
_____
_____

Names _____

Name-Calling and Critical Thinking

Tabloid Journalism

Tabloid newspapers, often seen in grocery stores, evoke negative feelings about people, particularly celebrities. While most people are aware that tabloid journalism is not necessarily factual, there is still a huge market for such newspapers.

An example of tabloid journalism that uses the name-calling technique might be a story about a government cover-up of a UFO sighting. In this article, the reader is persuaded to distrust the government because politicians are supposedly trying to hide the truth about UFOs landing in America. Words and phrases such as "government cover-up" and "hide the truth" are examples of name-calling.

With your group, study an article from a tabloid newspaper. Look for examples of name-calling in which the reader is persuaded to distrust or dislike someone or something. Using a colored highlighter, mark the words or phrases in the article that employ the name-calling technique. Record the words and phrases your group highlighted.

_____
_____
_____
_____
_____
_____
_____
_____
_____

What are the most negative things your group noticed about this article? _____
_____
_____
_____

Name _____

Integrating Name-Calling

Wanted!

Imagine that you are working in the area of criminal justice, and it is your responsibility to design "Wanted" posters of criminals. In the space below, design a wanted poster that includes the person's name and aliases, a specific description, a list of the person's crimes, and the amount of the reward.

NOTES TO THE TEACHER
Transfer

When using the persuasive technique of transfer, images and symbols that are respected and admired are associated with an item or idea. This is done in hopes that people will associate the trust and status they have for the image or symbol with the product or idea.

One of the most obvious examples of transfer can be seen in advertisements for political candidates. In a national election, the commercial might use images of famous monuments in Washington D. C., or in other cities, an American flag, or a bald eagle. These images and symbols appeal to patriotic Americans who love their country.

Companies use symbols that they hope transfer to their product. For example, Allstate Insurance says, "You're in good hands with Allstate," and they show a pair of strong hands. Prudential Insurance Company of America advertises to "Get a piece of the rock," and they show a large solid rock. This leads people to believe that they are a rock-solid company, since the strength of the rock is transferred to the company.

Quaker Oats uses a picture of an old Quaker to represent their company. The Quaker can be associated with pure, simple, and wholesome oats. Even now, with many different Quaker Instant Oatmeal flavors, the Quaker still represents pure wholesome goodness to consumers.

In much the same way, the image of a little red schoolhouse has come to mean a quality old-fashioned education. Educators and students see the image used repeatedly in schools and other school-related buildings, as well as in books and educational materials.

Let's Go Logo (page 50)
This activity is a great way to make a game out of learning to identify and understand the persuasive technique of transfer. Students browse through appropriate magazines and newspapers looking for company names and logos. They will cut out each company's name, as well as the company's logo. Each student will need at least five index cards and some glue. They will glue a company name on one side of each card and its logo on the other side.

Next, ask students to trade with their friends and guess the company name by looking at the logos. Students may be surprised at the power of advertising by how many they know. If students have trouble with the answers, remind them that the company's name is on the back of the card.

Catchy Cookbooks (page 51)

Cookbooks not only contain wonderful recipe ideas, but they also offer appetizing photographs as visuals to encourage people to prepare the dishes. Divide the class into groups of four. Have students read through appropriate magazines and cut out pictures of fine cuisine and prepared foods. Then have them glue their pictures onto blank pages. Next, tell the students to make up recipes that will go with their pictures. Students should use words that sound fresh and appetizing so that the potential cook would want to prepare the dish. Students should also give the dish an exciting title like Nachos Spectacular or Chocolate Decadence. Finally, have the students bind the pages together to make a group cookbook.

Follow-Up: Compile the recipes from each group's cookbook to make a class recipe book. Keep the book in the classroom library for students to check out. If time permits, encourage students to cook their favorite dishes and take photographs of the food they cooked. This would make an interesting recipe book.

Anchors Away (page 52)

People who own boats usually take naming them very seriously. Since different boats serve different purposes, a boat's name should reflect the purpose of the boat and the values of the owner. In this activity, 14 different types of boat are listed. Students will develop names for boats that relate to the purpose of the boat and the nature of the owner.

Hurray for the Holidays (page 53)

Holiday images and symbols shown in stores often encourage people to begin shopping for the holiday season. This activity asks students to brainstorm holiday symbols and images used by stores to encourage customers to buy gifts for their friends and loved ones.

Next, students are to think of two possible images that might be seen on a special gift for each person listed on the activity sheet. The images should reflect what the people do or who they are.

Pump Up! (page 54)
Mr. Bodybuilder sells goods and services for health-conscious people. He owns a gym and sells memberships, vitamins, etc. He makes presentations explaining and promoting a healthy lifestyle. But Mr. Bodybuilder needs visual images for his presentation! Students should consider what visual aids for a health and fitness presentation would transfer to the promotion of healthy habits, and develop a list of ideas.

Next, have students write a three-minute speech that Mr. Bodybuilder can use to effectively promote and sell memberships to his gym.

Follow-up: Let students share their three-minute speeches with the class. Discuss the persuasive nature of the speeches and the images of health and fitness that transfer to the potential customer.

Sizing Up Symbols (page 55)
Symbols and images represent meanings to us when we see them in our everyday lives. Meanings may vary slightly from person to person, but many symbols and images carry similar meanings to people. In this activity, popular symbols and images are listed, and each student is asked to write what each symbol means to him or her.

Bon Voyage! (page 56)
Travel agents often persuade people to arrange vacations. In a travel agent's office, one might see beautiful photographs of far away places, images that might draw us to a new place. For example, oranges can be used to lure people to Florida, cowboys are used to represent Texas, and basketball is associated with Indiana.

Ask students to pretend that they are travel agents and that they need to arrange vacations for their clients. Ask them to consider what images they might use to advertise various destinations. Students will write descriptions of the images for each destination.

Put Your Best Foot Forward (page 57)
While the persuasive technique of transfer is used mostly for positive images, it is occasionally used to show negative images. This is often done to discourage negative behavior.

In this activity, three positive personal habits and three negative personal habits are listed. Ask students to write descriptions of images that can be used to encourage the three positive personal habits, as well as descriptions of images that can be used to discourage negative personal habits.

Transfer and Critical Thinking (page 58)
Imagine that a school coach has started a new sports team at a nearby school. What will the team's name be? What will its logo and mascot look like?

Tell students that it is their responsibility to name the new team and develop a logo and a mascot. Announce a class contest to determine the name, logo, and mascot. Each student should create an entry for the contest. The name, logo, and mascot should be appropriate for the school and its location and should transfer positive images to the new team.

After all the entries are complete, the class can vote on the best name, logo, and mascot for the team.

Supplement: Instead of having a contest based on a new sports team, have one to find a name and a logo for a new school newspaper.

Integrating the Transfer Technique (page 59)
Have students pretend that they have just been knighted by King Arthur as knights of his round table. Each student must develop a coat of arms to place on his or her battleshield. There should be four sections in the coat of arms, with an image or symbol drawn in each section. The image should transfer positive feelings about the bearer's personality and good name.

Let's Go Logo

Companies use logos to sell products. These logos are often images or symbols that represent something that people associate with positive and respectful feelings.

Look through appropriate newspapers and magazines for pictures of logos associated with various company names. For example, look for items like the American Flag, the Statue of Liberty, the Liberty Bell, the bald eagle, a little red schoolhouse, or a church that are used in advertisements for a company's goods or services.

Cut out the logos and their company names. Glue each logo to one side of an index card and the company name to the other side. Make at least five cards.

Give your cards to some friends and see if they can guess the company names by looking at the logos. You may be surprised at the power of advertising!
Remember: The company name is written on the back of each logo card.

Name _____

Catchy Cookbooks

Cookbooks are known for giving us great recipes and tips for cooking. In addition, many cookbooks include beautiful photographs of prepared foods sprinkled with lovely garnishes and served on tasteful china.

Pictures in cookbooks serve an important purpose. They show how attractive a dish can be, encouraging you to prepare a certain recipe. We associate the pictures with our own cooking expertise, so that we are persuaded to try the recipe.

In groups of four, make a group cookbook. Look through magazines until you find taste-tempting photographs of food. Cut them out and paste them on a sheet of paper. Then write a mock recipe that goes with the picture. Be certain to use words that will sound fresh and appetizing so that the potential cook will want to prepare this dish. Give your recipe a fresh and appetizing name as well. For example, use descriptive words to make names such as Nachos Spectacular or Chocolate Decadence.

Compile your group's recipes and bind them into a group cookbook.

Name _____

Anchors Away

Many people own boats. Boats serve different purposes for different people. Some boats are for fishing or shrimping. Others are for water-skiing or recreation. Some people live on houseboats. There are cruise ships and pirate ships. A boat is usually named by its owner. The name chosen often relates to the boat's unique purpose or to the personality or values of the owner.

Listed below are different kinds of boats. Name each boat so that its name is appropriate for its purpose or owner.

1. Pirate ship _____
2. Cruise liner _____
3. Water-skiing boat _____
4. Sailboat _____
5. Catamaran _____
6. Houseboat _____
7. Shrimping boat _____
8. Fishing boat _____
9. Jet ski _____
10. Recreation boat _____
11. Rowboat _____
12. Tugboat _____
13. Canoe _____
14. Ferryboat _____

© Frank Schaffer Publications, Inc.   FS-10207 Persuasive Speaking and Writing

Name _____

Hurray for Holidays

When the holidays approach, stores and malls are adorned with beautiful decorations symbolizing the holidays that people celebrate. This kind of atmosphere encourages people to buy gifts for their friends and loved ones in order to celebrate the holidays. Customers transfer the warm feelings they get from seeing the decorations in the store to shopping for gifts.

In the space below, brainstorm all the possible images and symbols used by stores during the holidays to encourage customers to buy gifts for their friends and loved ones.

Holiday images and symbols: _____
_____
_____
_____

What images might you see on special gifts for the following people? Think of two images that could be associated with each person listed that would reflect what that person does, things he or she enjoys, and who the person is. For instance, an apple would be a gift image associated with a teacher.

A teacher   _____   _____
A doctor   _____   _____
Your sister   _____   _____
Your brother   _____   _____
Your mother   _____   _____
Your father   _____   _____

© Frank Schaffer Publications, Inc.　　　　　　FS-10207 Persuasive Speaking and Writing

Name _____

Pump Up!

Mr. Bodybuilder sells health goods and services related to healthy lifestyles. He owns a gym and sells memberships, vitamins, protein drinks, and workout clothes. He rents tanning beds to customers, offers aerobics classes, and provides the expertise of personal trainers.

Presentations are made by Mr. Bodybuilder to local businesses and organizations. In them, he explains the health products and services he has to offer.

Consider the symbols and images Mr. Bodybuilder could use as visual aids for his presentations. He would want images that would transfer positive images about healthful lifestyles. Develop a list of images that he could use for his visual aids.

_____   _____   _____
_____   _____   _____
_____   _____   _____

Write a three-minute speech that Mr. Bodybuilder could use at local businesses and organizations to promote his products and sell memberships in his gym.

_____
_____
_____
_____
_____
_____
_____
_____
_____
_____
_____
_____
_____
_____
_____
_____

Name _____

Sizing Up Symbols

Symbols and images represent meanings to us when we see them in our everyday lives. Meanings may vary slightly from person to person, but many symbols and images represent similar meanings to people.

Listed below are some popular symbols and images. Beside each symbol or image, write what it means to you.

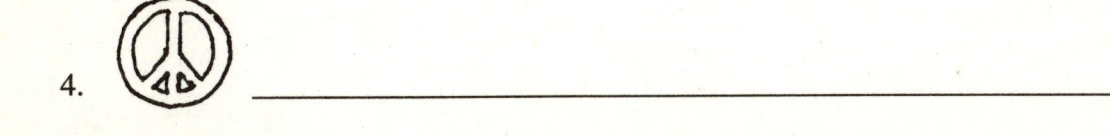

1. [$] _____
   _____

2.  [light bulb] _____
   _____

3.  [?] _____
   _____

4. [peace sign] _____
   _____

5.  [American flag] _____
   _____

6. [skull and crossbones] _____
   _____

© Frank Schaffer Publications, Inc.　　　55　　　FS-10207 Persuasive Speaking and Writing

Name _____

Bon Voyage!

Pretend that you are a travel agent, and that you arrange vacations for your clients. Of course, various symbols are used to represent different areas of the continent and the world. For example, oranges can be used to represent Florida, cowboys may be symbolic of Texas, and basketball is associated with Indiana.

Think about the symbols and images you would use if you wanted your clients to plan vacations to various destinations. Listed below are possible destinations. Describe the symbols you would use to encourage clients to plan vacations to these destinations.

1. Australia _____
_____

2. California _____
_____

3. the Caribbean _____
_____

4. the Orient _____
_____

5. Europe _____
_____

6. Alaska _____
_____

7. Hawaii _____
_____

8. Africa _____
_____

Challenge: Design a travel brochure for one of the destinations. Include symbols and illustrations.

Name _____

◫ Put Your Best Foot Forward

While the persuasive technique of transfer is used mostly in cases of positive images, it is sometimes used to show negative consequences as well. For example, a nonsmoking campaign shows a black and white photo of a tired older woman with crooked teeth and dark circles under her eyes. The caption says, "Smoking is glamorous."

Listed below are three positive personal habits and three negative personal habits.

Write descriptions of images that can be used to encourage the three positive personal habits and to discourage the three negative personal habits.

Positive Personal Habits   Encouraging Image Descriptions

1. Eating healthful foods   _____

2. Thoughtful study   _____

3. Exercise   _____

Negative Personal Habits   Discouraging Image Descriptions

1. Bullying   _____

2. Smoking   _____

3. Being a couch potato   _____

Name _____

Transfer and Critical Thinking

A school coach has started a new sports team at a nearby school. It is the responsibility of your class to name the team and develop a logo and a mascot.

The coach has decided to hold a contest to determine a name, logo, and mascot of the new team. Each student is invited to create an entry. The name, logo, and mascot should be appropriate for the school and its location, and should convey positive images that can be transferred to the team.

In the space below, give your idea for the team name. Then sketch your idea for the logo and the mascot. After all the entries are completed, your class can vote to select the name, logo, and mascot for the team.

Name _____

◧ *Integrating the Transfer Technique*

Pretend that you have just been knighted by King Arthur as a knight of his round table. It is your responsibility to develop a coat of arms to place on your battleshield. Decorate the coat of arms with a different symbol in each section. Include symbols that carry positive images about you and your good name.

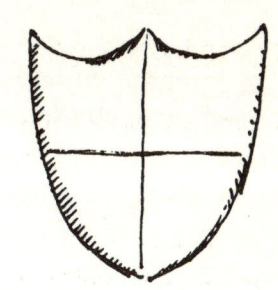

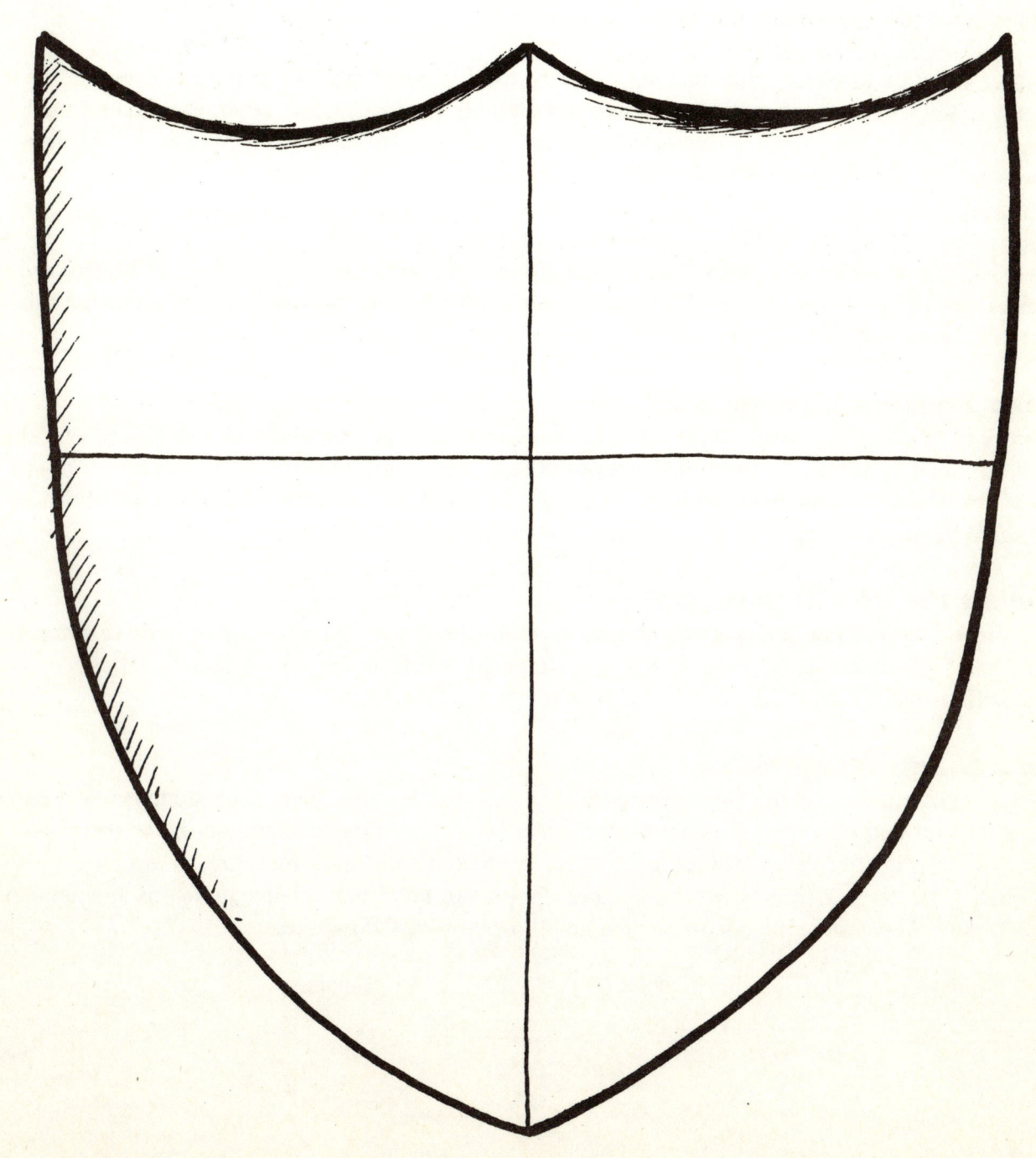

NOTES TO THE TEACHER

Card Stacking

Have you ever given all the good points about one side of an issue and all the bad points about the opposite side? This is called card stacking, or stacking the cards in your favor. Sometimes advertisements compare products, but it is important to check to see if the advertisers are being fair. Often a company's advertisement tells about all the advantages of its product and highlights the disadvantages of the competitor's product. Of course, the advertisement never describes any advantages of the competitor's product.

Another situation in which card stacking might be used is if children are trying to encourage their parents to get a cat rather than a dog. They might tell all the good things about cats and all the bad things about dogs. To be fair, of course, they would have to consider all the good and bad things about each choice before the family made the decision.

While card stacking may not be fair because it eliminates relevant information, it should be realized that it is a technique of persuasion that is used quite often. Sometimes people say, "The cards were stacked against me." After completing this chapter, it will become apparent to students what this quotation really means.

Pizza Preference (page 63)
In order to help students begin thinking in terms of card stacking, in which all the pros of one side are articulated versus all the cons of the opposite side, have them think about a popular food—pizza. On the activity sheet, students give the advantages of eating dinner at a pizza parlor. Then they give the disadvantages of eating dinner at a cafeteria-style restaurant.

Calling the Cards (page 64)
Talk shows seem to fascinate people, and various talk show hosts gain popularity with different audiences. Ask each student to select his or her favorite and least favorite television talk show personalities and to stack the cards in favor of his or her favorite.

Card Sharks (page 65)
Students will practice using card stacking through this oral activity. Have each student select one of two field trips and plan a brief speech to convince the class and the teacher why he or she chose that one. Let students chose between a shark aquarium and a dinosaur museum, or any two attractions that they wish. Students should present pros to favor their choice and cons against the other choice. Have them include three pros and three cons in their speeches.

Stacking Baseball Cards (page 66)
Divide the class into pairs. Each pair needs to select its favorite professional team sport. Once the sport is agreed upon, each individual chooses his or her favorite team in that sport. Next, each student stacks the cards in favor of his or her chosen team. Students will record and explain reasons why their team is the best. In addition, students will record and explain why their choice is a better choice than their partner's. As a follow-up activity, see if anyone was persuaded by his or her partner.

Card-iologist (page 67)
Cardiologists are physicians who specialize in the heart. These doctors also encourage people to eat healthful foods and to follow an exercise plan.

Invite students to research the positive health benefits of a healthful diet and a consistent exercise plan. Ask students to pretend that they are cardiologists who must convince their patients to lead a healthful lifestyle. Encourage students to document their research as they write what they will tell their patients in order to convince them to eat sensibly and to exercise. Invite students to share their advice with the class.

Ocean City or Mission to Mars? (page 68)
NASA plans to have an operable space station by 2001. What if its next project is a mission to Mars? There are other scientists and researchers who want to build a city on or under the ocean.

Divide the class into two groups, one group that wants to plan a mission to Mars and another that wants to build a city on or under the ocean. Each group should engage in thorough research on their topic, being careful to keep organized notes.

The goal of each group is to make a presentation in which it shows the benefits of the project it supports and the barriers to the other group's project. During the presentation, each group should use visual aids such as models or posters.

After the groups have made their presentations, each group will have an opportunity to engage in a timed rebuttal to defend its project. Following the rebuttals, the class can vote to determine the most feasible project.

Card Stacking and Critical Thinking (pages 69 and 70)
Divide the class into groups of four. Each group needs to select a topic from the list on page 62 or chose one that a group member suggests.

Two people from the group will argue for one side while the remaining two people argue for the other side. Each pair of students should develop its argument by brainstorming the positive points about its side and the negative points about the opposite side.

After both pairs have presented their arguments, they will have a timed rebuttal to defend their positions. Next, the group of four will vote to see if anyone in the group was persuaded to change sides.

The record sheet provided on page 70 provides an organized structure where students can record their topics, positive points, negative points, rebuttal comments, and results from the vote.

Card-Stacking Topics

Which is Better?

Morning shower versus evening shower
Bananas versus apples
Boating on rivers versus boating on lakes
String piano versus electric piano
Pens versus pencils
Television shows versus movies
Baseball versus basketball
Combination locks versus key locks
Smell of flowers versus smell of herbs

Integrating the Card-Stacking Technique (pages 71 and 72)

Find current opinion pages from newspapers that employ the card-stacking technique. Be certain to preview the articles before sharing them with the class.

Ask students to select topics that are noteworthy and of current interest from the opinion pages. Students should collect at least three articles on that topic from the opinion pages. These articles will be attached to the interview sheet (page 71).

Next, students should identify two people that they can interview on the topic. They can be experts, teachers, parents, students, or anyone who has formed an opinion on the topic. Have students formulate 10 interview questions about the topic and record them on the interview sheet.

Students will record responses from the interviews and their own comments about the interviews on the response sheet (page 72). As a result of the interviews, they may begin to see the topic in a new light.

Pizza Preference

After a day of work and school, you and your parents decide to go out together for supper. Your parents want to go to a cafeteria-style restaurant, where they feel there will be many different choices. On the other hand, you would prefer a pizza parlor, where all four food groups are represented on one slice of pizza. Develop a list of reasons why it would be a good idea to eat at the pizza parlor. Create a second list of reasons why you would NOT like to eat at a cafeteria. Be creative, and try to generate as many reasons as you can.

Pizza Pros

1. _____
2. _____
3. _____
4. _____
5. _____
6. _____
7. _____
8. _____
9. _____
10. _____

Cafeteria Cons

1. _____
2. _____
3. _____
4. _____
5. _____
6. _____
7. _____
8. _____
9. _____
10. _____

In the space below, describe the way your parents' might react to your persuasive effort. Where do you think they will decide to eat?

Name _____

■ Calling the Cards

Talk shows are becoming more and more popular, and it seems everyone has a favorite talk show host. Choose your favorite and least favorite television talk show hosts.

Next, stack the cards in favor of your favorite talk show host and against your least favorite talk show host. Develop a list of the pros for your talk show personality and the cons for your least favorite talk show personality.

Favorite Talk Show Host **Pros**	**Least Favorite Talk Show Host** **Cons**
Name _____	Name _____

Card Sharks

Pretend that your class has an opportunity to go on a field trip. You and your classmates must decide between a trip to a shark aquarium or a trip to a dinosaur museum. Each student must vote and explain why he or she is voting that way.

Write your explanation below. Try to incorporate the card-stacking technique of persuasion in your explanation and include three reasons that support your choice, and three reasons for NOT choosing the other option. Present your explanation to the class.

_____
_____
_____
_____
_____
_____
_____
_____
_____
_____
_____
_____
_____
_____
_____
_____
_____
_____
_____
_____
_____

© Frank Schaffer Publications, Inc.   FS-10207 Persuasive Speaking and Writing

Name _____

Stacking Baseball Cards

Find a partner. With your partner, select a favorite professional team sport. You should each choose a team from the competitive sport that the two of you agree upon. For example, if you and your partner select baseball, then one of you might choose the Cubs and the other might choose the Reds.

Try to persuade your partner that your team is better. To do this, write down and explain the outstanding qualities of your team. Then explain why your choice is a better choice than your partner's choice. For example, you might comment on your team's nice playing field and the wonderful hot dogs that they serve. You might make negative comments about the mascot of your partner's team or about the uncomfortable bleachers in the stadium.

Record your ideas on the lines below.

Favorite Competitive Team Sport: _____

Your favorite team in the chosen sport: _____

Reasons why your team is the best: _____
_____
_____
_____
_____
_____
_____
_____

Your partner's favorite team: _____

Reasons why your partner's favorite team is NOT the best choice: _____
_____
_____
_____
_____
_____
_____
_____

Card-iologist

Cardiologists are physicians who specialize in the heart and its functions. They work with patients to help them stay healthy. Among other things, cardiologists encourage their patients to eat healthful foods and to maintain an exercise plan.

Research the positive health benefits of a healthful diet and a consistent exercise plan.

Pretend that you are a cardiologist and you must convince your patients to eat right and exercise. Think about what you will tell them based on the benefits that you found through your research and experience. Write a summary of what you would tell your patients. Share your summary with the class.

_____
_____
_____
_____
_____
_____
_____
_____
_____
_____
_____
_____
_____
_____
_____
_____
_____
_____
_____
_____

Ocean City or Mission to Mars?

Scientists have ideas for exploring the unknown. NASA plans to have an operable space station by 2001. Then it hopes to investigate Mars. Other researchers believe that we could have a city on or under the ocean.

Your class will work in two groups. One group will plan a mission to Mars and the other group will plan the construction of an ocean city. Your group must research its topic thoroughly and be able to tell about the benefits of such a project. Try to include vivid descriptions of the future to help everyone imagine your project. Use the space at the bottom of this page to take notes of ideas or descriptions that you want to include. Be sure to point out the disadvantages and problems of the other group's project as well as the advantages of yours. In other words, your group needs to stack the cards for your side.

Present your project to the class through a speech and visual aids such as models or posters of the project. After both presentations, each group has an opportunity to engage in a timed rebuttal to defend its project. Then take a class vote to determine which project should be undertaken.

Planning

_____
_____
_____
_____
_____
_____
_____
_____
_____
_____
_____
_____

Card Stacking and Critical Thinking

Work in groups of four. Each group should select a topic from the list below, or choose one that a group member suggests.

Two people from your group will argue for one side and the other two will argue for the opposing side. Remember to develop your argument by using the card-stacking technique, that is by giving the positive points about your side and the negative points about the other. Brainstorm with your partner to develop points for your argument.

After both sides in your group have presented their viewpoints, each side may have a two-minute rebuttal. Finally, the group will vote on the stronger viewpoint.

Record your work on the record sheet found on page 70. Include your topic choice, positive points about your topic, negative points about the opposing topic, the rebuttal comments, and the results of the vote.

Card-Stacking Topics

Which is better?

    Morning shower versus evening shower

    Bananas versus apples

    Boating on rivers versus boating on lakes

    String piano versus electric piano

    Pens versus pencils

    Television shows versus movies

    Baseball versus basketball

    Combination locks versus key locks

    Smell of flowers versus smell of herbs

Name _____

Record Sheet for Card Stacking

Topic Choice for Group: _____

Your viewpoint: _____

Positive Points   Negative Points
(for your viewpoint)   (against your opponent's viewpoint)

_____   _____
_____   _____
_____   _____
_____   _____
_____   _____
_____   _____
_____   _____
_____   _____
_____   _____
_____   _____
_____   _____
_____   _____

Rebuttal Comments (Two minutes!): _____
_____
_____
_____
_____
_____
_____
_____

Vote Results: _____

© Frank Schaffer Publications, Inc.   FS-10207 Persuasive Speaking and Writing

Name _____

Interview Questions

Collect current newspapers and read the opinion pages. Look for the card-stacking technique used in the articles. Determine a topic of interest, collect at least three articles about it, and attach the articles to this sheet.

Next, identify two people that you can interview on the topic. They can be experts, teachers, parents, students, or anyone who has formed an opinion on the topic.

Formulate at least 10 interview questions concerning the topic. List your questions on the lines below. Record your interview responses and your comments about the interview on the the record sheet found on page 72. You will need a copy of the record sheet for each person that you interview.

Interview Questions

1. _____
2. _____
3. _____
4. _____
5. _____
6. _____
7. _____
8. _____
9. _____
10. _____

Write a letter to a newspaper giving your opinion about the topic you chose.

© Frank Schaffer Publications, Inc.   FS-10207 Persuasive Speaking and Writing

Name _____

Interview Response Sheet

Response to Question 1: _____
_____

Response to Question 2: _____
_____

Response to Question 3: _____
_____

Response to Question 4: _____
_____

Response to Question 5: _____
_____

Response to Question 6: _____
_____

Response to Question 7: _____
_____

Response to Question 8: _____
_____

Response to Question 9: _____
_____

Response to Question 10: _____
_____

Comments about the interview: _____
_____
_____

NOTES TO THE TEACHER
Testimonial

Testimonials are a widely used vehicle for persuading people. Testimonials build on the excitement that a celebrity brings out in people. An advertiser or a fund raiser for an organization may hire a celebrity to endorse its product or cause. People may buy the product or give a donation because the celebrity endorses it, even if the celebrity does not actually use the product or financially support the cause. If people like the celebrity, they will like the product or organization as well.

There are many examples of using testimonials in order to persuade. Mary Lou Retton gives a big grin on a cereal box, Ray Charles sings about a soft drink, Michael Jordan sports a brand of athletic shoes, and Whitney Houston sings with her true voice through telephone lines.

Political campaigns sometimes make use of celebrity testimonials. A political candidate may have a celebrity speak out about his or her character or qualifications. The celebrity may support the political platform developed by the candidate. People who like and respect the celebrity often transfer these feelings to the political candidate.

Television Testimonials (page 75)
Television commercials include many examples of testimonials involving celebrities. Give students copies of the worksheet for this activity. On it, have them record five examples of testimonials that they see as they watch television. Have them include the name of the celebrity, the reason the celebrity is famous, and the product, company, or organization being represented.

Let's Look for Links! (page 76)
Tape five television commercials that include examples of testimonials and show them to the class. Point out that some celebrities involved have a logical relationship with the product, company, or organization they are representing, but that others do not. For example, Michael Jordan may have an obvious relationship with a company that makes athletic shoes since he is an athlete. On the other hand, when a celebrity gives testimony to a cereal, a soft drink, or a telephone company, he or she may have little or no experience with the product.

Pushing Pasta (page 77)
Ask the students to choose a famous actor or actress and write a script of what that celebrity might say to advertise a product called Spectacular Spaghetti Sauce. Each student should consider what special things a celebrity might say that would allow his or her personality to show through and that would also encourage consumers to buy the product.

Famous Faces (page 78)
Provide magazines and ask students to find and cut out five examples of testimonials. They should glue the cutouts on a sheet of construction paper to make a collage. On the activity sheet, students should write the name of the celebrity, why he or she is famous, and the name of the product, company, or organization he or she is representing.

Testimonials and Critical Thinking (page 79)
Discuss the continuing popularity of restaurants that emphasize famous people and celebrities. The Hard Rock Cafe, Planet Hollywood, and the Michael Jordan restaurant in Chicago are all examples. Conduct a class discussion about why celebrities might own restaurants and why people go to them. Instruct the students to consider various perspectives and write thoughtful answers to the questions on the activity sheet.

Integrating the Testimonial Technique (page 80)
Ask the students to design a testimonial advertising campaign in which they select a product they want to sell, choose a celebrity who will speak about the product, and explain why that celebrity will be persuasive for consumers.

Name _____

Television Testimonials

Many examples of testimonial persuasion can be found in television commercials. Well-known people speak out about certain products or organizations. Advertisers know that celebrities who are respected and well-liked can encourage people to buy products or support certain organizations.

Next time you sit down to watch television, listen for examples of the use of testimonials. Write down five examples of testimonials. For each, include the name of the celebrity, the reasons the celebrity is famous, and the product, company, or organization the celebrity is representing.

      Celebrity   Reason Celebrity Is Famous   Product, Company, or Organization

1. _____ _____ _____

2. _____ _____ _____

3. _____ _____ _____

4. _____ _____ _____

5. _____ _____ _____

Name _____

🔲 *Let's Look for Links!*

Sometimes there are connections between celebrities and the products they are selling, but sometimes there are not. For instance, Michael Jordan may be able to sell athletic shoes effectively because everyone knows that he has a lot of experience with athletic shoes. On the other hand, when a celebrity gives testimony to a cereal, a soft drink, or a telephone company, he or she may have little or no experience with the product.

Watch the testimonial television commercials shown by your teacher during class. Look for connections between the celebrity and the product, company, or organization. If there is a connection, write YES in the blank, and explain how they are related. If there is not a connection, write NO. Be certain to include the celebrity's name, and the product, company, or organization.

Celebrity   Product and Company or Organization

1. _____   _____

2. _____   _____

3. _____   _____

4. _____   _____

5. _____   _____

Relationship or Connection   Explanation

1. _____   _____

2. _____   _____

3. _____   _____

4. _____   _____

5. _____   _____

© Frank Schaffer Publications, Inc.   FS-10207 Persuasive Speaking and Writing

Pushing Pasta

Think of a famous actor or actress. Now imagine that celebrity selling Spectacular Spaghetti Sauce. How would he or she sell Spectacular Spaghetti Sauce? What special things would the celebrity say that would allow his or her personality to show through and encourage consumers to buy the product?

Write a testimonial for Spectacular Spaghetti Sauce to be given by a famous actor or actress.

Name of Actor or Actress: _____

Testimonial: _____

_____
_____
_____
_____
_____
_____
_____
_____
_____
_____
_____
_____
_____
_____
_____
_____
_____
_____
_____

Famous Faces

Magazine advertisements often feature testimonials that persuade us to do or believe something. Miss America may be seen with a milk mustache to convince us to drink milk. Famous people endorse products or organizations in magazine pictorials.

Flip through the pages of magazines to find five examples of testimonials. Cut them out and glue them to a sheet of construction paper to make a collage.

On the lines below, write the name of each celebrity, why he or she is famous, and the name of the product, company, or organization being advertised.

Celebrity	Reason Celebrity Is Famous	Product, Company, or Organization
1. _____	_____	_____
2. _____	_____	_____
3. _____	_____	_____
4. _____	_____	_____
5. _____	_____	_____

Name _____

Testimonials and Critical Thinking

Restaurants that are owned or promoted by celebrities are continuing to gain popularity. The Hard Rock Cafe, Planet Hollywood, and Michael Jordan's in Chicago are a few examples. Each of these restaurants features decor that is based on the celebrity's career, interests, or accomplishments.

What makes celebrities want to own or promote such restaurants? Why do people go to them? Is it because of the excellent food that is served or do people like the atmosphere of fame and fortune? Answer the following questions, trying to think of your answers from several different perspectives.

Why do celebrities own or promote restaurants?

_____
_____
_____
_____
_____
_____
_____

Why do people patronize celebrity restaurants?

_____
_____
_____
_____
_____
_____

Plan a restaurant that your favorite celebrity might open. Include the type of decor the celebrity would choose and name several food specialties that might be on the menu.

_____
_____
_____
_____
_____
_____

Name _____

Integrating the Testimonial Technique

Imagine that you are in charge of advertising at a company. Select a product to be sold by your company. Design an advertising campaign using a testimonial. Identify the audience your advertising campaign will target. Discuss who will speak and why he or she will be persuasive.

Product name and company that your advertising campaign will represent:
_____
_____

Audience that you will target:
_____
_____

Your celebrity: _____

Explain why you chose this celebrity. Why will he or she be persuasive?
_____
_____
_____
_____
_____
_____

Think of a product that is currently promoted by a celebrity. Identify the product and the celebrity. Then think of another celebrity who might do a better job of promoting the product. Explain why he or she would be a better spokesperson for the product.
_____
_____
_____
_____
_____
_____
_____

> NOTES TO THE TEACHER

Just Plain Folks

The "Just Plain Folks" technique makes use of the similarities of people. Things that people have in common, such as good, old-fashioned values like loving your mother, are the foundation of this technique.

People trust regular folks, so companies and politicians work very hard to make connections between regular folks and themselves. Advertisers that ask people to notice "country goodness" or "good, old-fashioned taste" are using this technique.

Telephone companies have made commercials in which families are brought closer together through the telephone lines. Since people all experience calling their families on the telephone, they believe that the company identifies with them.

Some companies advertise themselves as "little." A growing company might decide to emphasize how small it is by saying, "We eat all we can and sell the rest." Consumers might hear that and believe that they are getting a fresher, homemade product.

Politicians also make use of the plain-folks technique. They wear hard hats and go with workers to their job sites. They hold town meetings, or wear coveralls to go with a farmer's family to see their land. Politicians want to be seen as average people with the same values as regular folks.

Clothing Promotion (page 83)
Ask students to notice the styles and brands of the clothes they are wearing and to consider the popularity of various clothing brands and styles. Invite students to think about what they would say about their clothing in order to promote it using a plain-folks technique.

Just Plain Magazines (page 84)
Encourage students to look through old magazines to find five examples of this persuasive technique. Some examples will be found in advertisements and others will be found in articles. Have students glue their five examples to a sheet of construction paper to make a collage. Ask students to share their collages in groups of four. Students will explain why their examples are good choices.

Product Vignettes (page 85)
Ask students to select a company that markets products they really enjoy, perhaps from the fashion or food industries. Each student will compose a vignette (short scene) that would encourage others to buy the company's products.

Billboard Break (page 86)
Have students plan billboard signs for the products they promoted in their product vignettes. Encourage them to appeal to the values of just plain folks. Have them each select a slogan and suggest a photograph to use for the product and company. Ask the students to write detailed descriptions of their billboard photographs and slogans.

Soda Pop Interviews (page 87)
Students will ask their families to decide on the family's favorite soda pop. Next, students will interview their family members individually to learn their reasons for purchasing and drinking the family's favorite. Students will record on the record sheet each family member's reasons.

Telephone Talk (page 88)
Students will assume that they work for a telephone and communications company. They will be in charge of a new commercial that must appeal to a large audience through the just-plain-folks technique of persuasion. The commercial will appeal to more people if the experiences in the commercial are common to all people. Have students decide how they will stage the commercial. Then have them select the characters and setting, and write a script.

Just Plain Laundry (page 89)
Ask students to imagine that they are creating a commercial to sell All Clean Laundry Detergent. Each student must coordinate a commercial in which three people speak on behalf of All Clean Laundry Detergent. Students will write what each of the people will say to promote the product. Encourage students to include both males and females in their commercials.

Just Plain Folks and Critical Thinking: Which Came First? (page 90)
Ask students to consider the popularity of an item and the positive response of that item by average folks. Sometimes fads and trends begin by being popular with the wealthy people and then filter down to average people. Sometimes an item is popular regionally and then develops a more widespread popularity among average folks in other areas. Ask students to think of the trends that lead to the popularity of items such as ethnic foods, backpacks, fashions, and organic foods.

Integrating the Just-Plain-Folks Technique (page 91)
Have you ever noticed that a small company may advertise that it has the most famous product of its kind? On the other hand, a large company may emphasize aspects of its product that are associated with a small business. In this activity, students consider two pizza places. One is an example of a small pizza restaurant and the other is an example of a large, national pizza chain. Students must create slogans that reflect this trend to advertise both pizza places.

Clothing Promotion

Consider the pants, skirt, dress, or jeans that you are wearing right now. What is the brand name? Do any of your friends wear the same brand? Would you consider the brand name popular?

How would you speak about your clothing on behalf of the company that made it? If you were asked to be a spokesperson for the clothing company, what would you say that would encourage other people to buy that brand? Use the just-plain-folks technique of persuasion.

Brand name of clothing: _____

What would you say to sell the clothing? _____

Name _____

Just Plain Magazines

Look through old magazines to find five examples of the just-plain-folks technique of persuasion. The examples may not be only in the advertisements, although you will find many there. You may also see photographs in a news magazine of politicians who are using the technique. In magazines about Hollywood personalities, you may also see some image building through the use of the technique.

After you have found five examples in magazines, cut them out and glue them onto a sheet of construction paper to make a collage. On the lines below, write the reason why each example is a good choice. In groups of four, share your collage and explain your choices.

1. _____
   _____
   _____

2. _____
   _____
   _____

3. _____
   _____
   _____

4. _____
   _____
   _____

5. _____
   _____
   _____

Pretend that a presidential candidate is coming to visit your town. Where could he go to use the just-plain-folks technique in an attempt to gain the support of the people?

Name _____

Product Vignettes

Select a company that sells a product that you really enjoy. You may want to choose a company in the fashion industry or a company that sells food products. Compose a vignette (a short scene) that would encourage others to buy the company's product. Write it below.

Company name: _____

Your favorite product(s): _____
_____

Vignette: _____

Billboard Break

Billboards are a popular way to advertise. Big pictures with lights shining on them are popular in cities and along rural highways.

Use the company and product that you selected for the activity on page 85. Consider how you could be photographed with the product in a way that would promote the product. What would the slogan be? Write a description of the billboard photograph and the slogan idea on the lines below.

Company name and product: _____

Describe the photograph that will be used on the billboard: _____

Slogan for the billboard: _____

Name _____

Soda Pop Interviews

Ask your family members to decide what is the family's favorite soda pop. Once the favorite has been determined, imagine that you are in charge of putting together a commercial to promote it. Plan a commercial that will use your family to persuade people to buy that soda pop.

Interview the members of your family (either immediate or extended) and have them give their reasons for purchasing and drinking the family's favorite soda pop. Some of their comments may be appropriate to use in a just-plain-folks commercial.

What is your family's favorite brand of soda pop? _____

Record the reasons each family member gives for purchasing and drinking that kind of soda pop. (Continue on the back if necessary.)

Name: _____
_____
_____

Name: _____
_____
_____

Name: _____
_____
_____

Name: _____
_____
_____

Name: _____
_____
_____

© Frank Schaffer Publications, Inc.   FS-10207 PERSUASIVE SPEAKING AND WRITING

Name _____

Telephone Talk

Assume that you are working for a telephone and communications company. You are in charge of planning a new commercial. The commercial must appeal to a large audience and use the just-plain-folks technique of persuasion. The commercial will appeal to more people if it involves an experience (such as calling relatives and friends) that is common to all people.

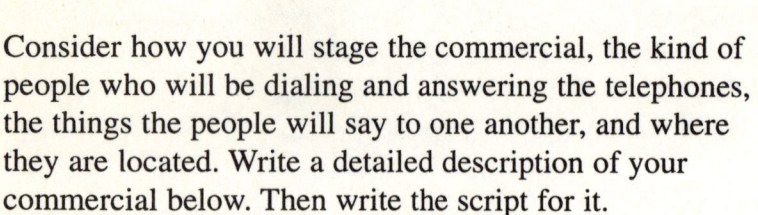

Consider how you will stage the commercial, the kind of people who will be dialing and answering the telephones, the things the people will say to one another, and where they are located. Write a detailed description of your commercial below. Then write the script for it.

_____
_____
_____
_____
_____
_____
_____
_____
_____
_____
_____
_____
_____
_____
_____
_____
_____
_____
_____
_____
_____
_____
_____
_____

Just Plain Laundry

We have all seen commercials in which a person is promoting a certain laundry detergent. The people in detergent commercials are persuasive because they seem like average people with laundry concerns that are similar to the concerns of a typical consumer. In short, the characters seem believable.

Pretend that you are selling All Clean Laundry Detergent. You have commitments from three people to speak on behalf of your product. You must write what each of the three people will say to promote your product.

First Person: _____
_____
_____
_____
_____
_____
_____

Second Person: _____
_____
_____
_____
_____
_____
_____

Third Person: _____
_____
_____
_____
_____
_____
_____

Just Plain Folks and Critical Thinking: Which Came First?

Sometimes fads and trends begin by being popular with wealthy people and then filter down to average people. Sometimes an item is popular regionally and then develops a more widespread popularity among average folks in other areas. Think of the trends that led to the popularity of the items listed below. Explain.

Ethnic Foods: _____
_____
_____
_____

Backpacks: _____
_____
_____
_____

Fashions: _____
_____
_____
_____

Organic Foods: _____
_____
_____
_____

Computer Games: _____
_____
_____
_____

Name _____

Integrating the Just-Plain-Folks Technique

Have you ever noticed how a small company may advertise that it has the most famous product of its kind or in the area? On the other hand, a large company may emphasize aspects of its products that are associated with a small business.

For example, one pizza restaurant is a small family business whose owners want to advertise that it has the best pizza in the country. Another pizza restaurant is part of a large chain. Its manager wants people to think they will receive the good quality and service often given by small companies.

Think of catchy names for the two pizza restaurants. Then create several slogans to advertise each.

Name of small family pizza restaurant: _____
Slogans: _____
_____
_____
_____
_____
_____
_____
_____

Name of large pizza chain: _____
Slogans: _____
_____
_____
_____
_____
_____
_____
_____

NOTES TO THE TEACHER
Tips for Writing a Persuasive Essay

In planning a persuasive essay, encourage each student to fill in a web to record his or her opinion on the topic and his or her reasons for supporting that opinion. Supporting details should be included.

Students should also identify the audience they are trying to reach and consider possible objections of the audience, particularly on a controversial topic. In addition to considering possible objections, students should formulate reasons why the audience should reject such objections. Students can think of other reasons to convince the audience as well. These are important beginning steps in writing a persuasive essay.

In the introduction of a persuasive essay, the writer should state his or her position, compliment the reader, state the sources of information used, and request that the reader maintain an open mind on the issue.

The body of the essay should include the author's reasons for supporting the opinion. Each reason should have relevant supporting details that further support the opinion and help persuade the reader.

The conclusion of the essay should feature a restatement of the author's position along with a request that the reader thoughtfully consider the writer's position.

Give each student a copy of the persuasive writing chart (page 93) when he or she is ready to plan a persuasive essay. The chart is an effective visual aid that students can use to organize their thinking.

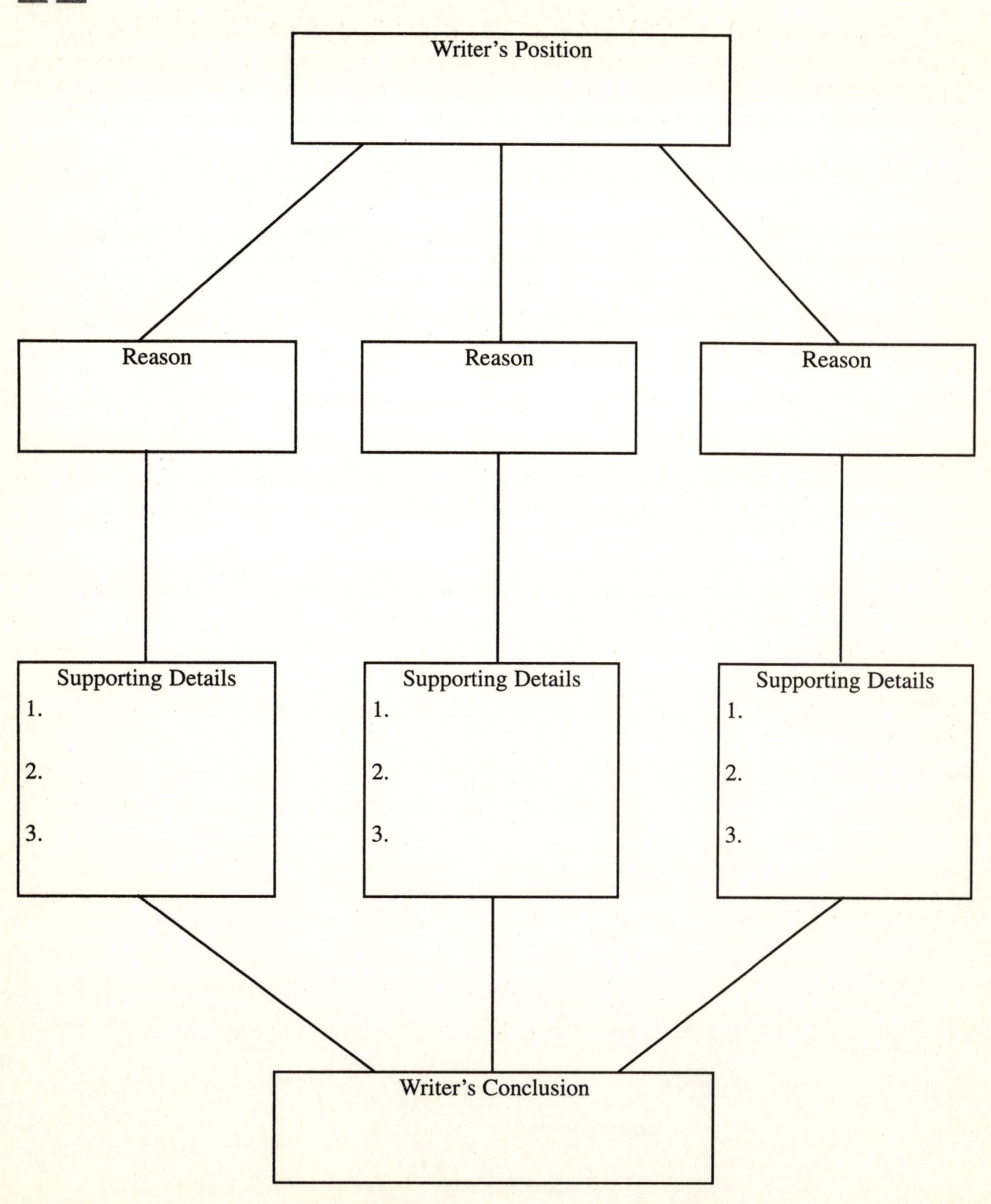

Name _____

Persuasive Writing Chart

```
                    ┌─────────────────┐
                    │ Writer's Position│
                    └─────────────────┘
                   /         |         \
        ┌────────┐    ┌────────┐    ┌────────┐
        │ Reason │    │ Reason │    │ Reason │
        └────────┘    └────────┘    └────────┘
            |             |             |
┌───────────────────┐ ┌───────────────────┐ ┌───────────────────┐
│ Supporting Details│ │ Supporting Details│ │ Supporting Details│
│ 1.                │ │ 1.                │ │ 1.                │
│ 2.                │ │ 2.                │ │ 2.                │
│ 3.                │ │ 3.                │ │ 3.                │
└───────────────────┘ └───────────────────┘ └───────────────────┘
                   \         |         /
                    ┌─────────────────┐
                    │Writer's Conclusion│
                    └─────────────────┘
```

Name _____

◨ *Organizing With Index Cards*

Show students how to organize an outline for a persuasive essay on multi-colored index cards. Have them use three colors to represent the three parts of the essay—the writer's position (one card), the writer's reasons for supporting the position (three or more cards), and the supporting details that strengthen the writer's reasons (as many cards as needed).

Explain to the students that they can arrange their color-coded cards in a hierarchy, placing the writer's position card at the top, the reason cards beneath the writer's position card, and the supporting detail cards at the base of the layout, below the appropriate reason cards. Then students can manipulative the parts of this movable outline until they are satisfied with it.

After students have completed their color-coded outlines, they can begin to write their persuasive essays based on information from the outline.